"This is wonderful Kimberly *has laid* ~~out what needs to be done~~ *before death--a thing we know is part of life here on earth."*

Vanessa Davis Griggs
Author of the Blessed Trinity series
Irondale, Alabama

***

"As a legal professional for over ten years, I must say this unique and comprehensive guide is truly a Godsend! Kimberly meticulously addresses all areas: personal, business, and spiritual in an easy-to-understand step-by-step format that takes the pain out of a traditionally painstaking experience. Follow this guide. Encourage your loved ones to follow this guide. Your families will be grateful. Your lawyers will be appreciative. And you will be able to rest knowing that you are leaving behind one of the greatest blessings of all - Peace and Order."

The Honorable Cheryl R. Bias, Esq.
Municipal Court Judge
Houston, Texas

***

"Although everyone knows death is inevitable, some fail to make the necessary preparations to leave things in proper order for their loved ones, not because they don't want to, but often they don't know how to. This book serves as a great guide to help many to properly prepare, with ease, for their time of departure."

Dr. Aretha Wilson
Educator, Author, Mentor, and CEO
Pastor of Kingdom Ambassadors Global Ministries
Lynbrook, New York

***

"In serving as a church administrator, I have seen first-hand how families are left in turmoil and devastation during times of loss and grief. Often, there is no knowledge of our loved ones last wishes or financial state of affairs. In this book, Kimberly has written steps from start to finish, taking away the fear and morbidity of this task, to leave Peace and Order."

Cheryl Ray
CFO and Church Administrator
Angie Ray Ministries – Church On The Rock
Matteson, Illinois

***

*"Ask yourself this question: Do I have my house in order and does my family or friends know my wishes once I transition from this earth to eternity? **Leaving Peace and Order** is Kimberly Graves' answer to this question when it is time to make decisions about your loved one's wishes as they prepare for transition from Earth. This book addresses what we must face. It takes us from an insecure place to a secure place where we won't have to worry about the wishes of our loved ones and where this information is stored. This book was written to address the specific realities faced by many people today. Kimberly offers simple and detailed solutions as to how to prepare before the time comes. Kimberly answers the questions: 1) What should I do next? 2) How do I get started? 3) Where do I find this information? 4) What information do I need? 5) Where and how do I store this information?*

***Leaving Peace and Order**, in every sense, teaches us and future generations on matters of vital importance to us all."*

Sandra S. Jordan
FDIC Tri-Four Funeral Home
Dallas, Texas

***

LEAVING PEACE AND ORDER

Step-By-Step Guide To Getting Your Affairs In Order

LEAVING PEACE & ORDER

KIMBERLY IVORY GRAVES

Step-by-step guide
to getting your
affairs in order

Unless otherwise indicated, all scripture quotations are from the King James Version of the Bible.

Leaving Peace and Order
Published by:
Kimberly Graves
Ivory's Possibilities
PO Box 9012
Gurnee, Illinois 60031

ISBN 978-0-9906436-0-9 (print book)
ISBN 978-0-9906436-1-6 (eBook)

Cover Design by Para Designers Inc.

Printed in the United States of America

DEDICATION

I dedicate this guide to the memory of two very special women who aided in shaping me into the woman that I am today.

The first woman is my loving mother, Ruth Ridley, who went home to be with the Lord in October 2012. She loved and nurtured me and my cousin Amy. She was the epitome of a woman of strength and great faith. My mother was my inspiration for writing this book. Her example is one of *Leaving Peace and Order*. She left one of the most important gifts a loved one could leave for his or her family. That gift was that she had her affairs in order before she went home to be with the Lord, which made her transition for our family a little bit easier. I will always cherish my mom's love and memories and will attempt to exemplify her strength and faith in my life.

The second woman is Dr. Angie Ray, who went home to be with the Lord in December 2005. She was instrumental in depositing biblical foundational truths into my life on which I stand today. Her love for God and His people left an indelible impression on my life. Dr. Ray also allowed me to be a ghost writer for many of her earlier published books. I count it an honor to have served such a remarkable woman of God.

***

ACKNOWLEDGMENTS

I am grateful to my Lord and Savior, Jesus Christ, who makes it possible for me to live life abundantly, and eventually, life eternally with Him.

Love and appreciation to Douglas E. Graves, my darling husband, who stands by my side encouraging me in whatever endeavor I choose. I am grateful to you for being there for me when my mom went home to be with the Lord. Also, thank you for your love and encouragement throughout the process of this book project.

I would like to express sincere appreciation to my wonderful family, the 'Ivy Vine', who was also there for me when my mother was ill and during her final transition. Amy, AmBree, 'Chappy', Armorie and Leon, Christine and Thomas, Annie,

Ebbert, Linda and to all my cousins – I love you all! Special love to the Jordan family – my father Willie, Rick and Sandra, Mary Frances, Allison, Rebecca, Ken and Cookie, Angel, Steven, Sandra, Hiawatha and the rest of the Jordan gang!

Thank you, Pastor Kimberly Ray Gavin, the Ray sisters and that great "Church on the Rock" for your love, prayers and support. – I love you so much!

I would be remiss if I did not mention my best friend, Cheryl Ray, who pushed me until this project was completed. Thank you Cheryl for the push! And to the rest of the 'BFFers': Precious, Michelle, LaWanda and Kristie – thank you for your friendship and support – love you girls forever.

Fay Bonds, Delphia Esters, Earlene Langston, Leon Lee, Regina McNeal, LaWanda Rucker, Marsha Somppi, Shalanda Spencer, Denice Stitt,

Teri Tatum, and Precious Washington – You added that special touch to this guide. Thank you so much for candidly sharing your personal experiences. I am appreciative!

I am grateful for the wonderful individuals who endorsed this guide. Many blessings bestowed upon Pastor Jace Cox, Vanessa Davis Griggs, Dr. Aretha Wilson, Cheryl Ray, Cynthia Harris, Armorie Lee, Sandra S. Jordan, Louise Wicks, Delphia Esters and The Honorable Cheryl R. Bias. Thank you for believing in and supporting me.

Prophetess Patricia Garland and Dr. Aretha Wilson, thank you both for prophetically speaking into my life concerning writing books.

Sincere appreciation expressed to Karolyn BoBo, Pamela Haney, Michelle Johnson, Michelle Moton, Cindy Reeve, Lola Scheltens, and Denice Stitt, who gave of their precious time to proof and edit this guide. Thank you Ladies!

Mari Baskin, Para Designers Inc., special thanks to you for coming to my rescue and designing the cover.

Thank you to everyone who shared their thoughts, love and encouragement to make this guide my masterpiece.

Finally, a special thank you to YOU for purchasing this guide, my prayer is that you utilize it to its fullest and *Leave Peace and Order* for your loved ones.

**

TABLE OF CONTENTS

CHAPTER SIX

CHAPTER SEVEN

CHAPTER EIGHT

CHAPTER NINE

FOREWORD

It is very important to think about what will happen upon one's demise. This publication, *Leaving Peace and Order*, answers many of the questions confronting loved ones who are left behind such as: What special wishes need to be honored? What funeral home to use? What cemetery should be used? Where are the insurance papers? Where are the passwords to important websites that house personal records and other pertinent information? All of these questions and so many others should be considered while one is in sound mind and capable of making very important decisions. This resource serves as a guide and addresses issues in helping to complete pre-burial plans and provides opportunities for survivors who are left to handle the business of loved ones and friends with ease.

The author of *Leaving Peace and Order*, Mrs. Kimberly Graves, is such an unselfish person. She is one who desires to help as many persons as she can by issuing this publication. As you navigate through this guide, you will soon appreciate the time, effort and research that was done by Mrs. Graves to help others even as they face decisions pertaining to death.

When I discovered that Mrs. Graves had written a book, I immediately began reflecting on the first time I met her. During the summer of 2004, a group of my church members from North Carolina accompanied me to Angie Ray Ministries - The Church on the Rock in Matteson, Illinois and upon our arrival, one of the first persons we met was the former Kimberly Ivory, now Graves. This lady had coordinated an early morning breakfast and did not hesitate to assist us with whatever we needed while we were visiting the ministry.

Today, some ten years later, Mrs. Graves is still seeking to help others wherever she can.

It is evident that Mrs. Graves knows firsthand how important it is to approach death intelligently and peacefully. This book is not the average book but an effective guide birthed out of experience to assist in getting all documents in place while one is competent and before one transitions from this earthly life to the eternal. This tool is an unselfish one that will cause the Administrator/Executor assigned to handling others affairs, to do so in an honorable, peaceful and orderly manner.

Dr. Jace L. Cox
Founder/Pastor
Liberty Praise Center
Sanford, North Carolina

***

INTRODUCTION

Have you ever lost a loved one and did not know the first thing to do? Did you wish you knew what they desired? Were you frustrated when you could not readily put your hands on their important documents? Had you hoped they would have left specific instructions or directives? If you have not, I am sure there is someone you know who has expressed these frustrations. The loss of someone near and dear to you can be devastating. The hopelessness and despair is very real. The added stress of having to make final arrangements can be overwhelming. Even so, many of these stresses can be eliminated by having all the important documents and directives needed to grant one's final wishes.

Leaving Peace and Order is a book to guide you through steps of getting your affairs in order now, so that when you transition from time to eternity, you can leave your family with peace of mind during their time of sorrow. The loss of a loved one is extremely distressing, and grief and sorrow can be almost unbearable. Yet, having one's affairs in order can make a world of difference and supply peace even in the midst of sorrow. You have the opportunity of *Leaving Peace and Order* for your family. Taking the time now to get your affairs in order will provide the support your family will need to carry out your final wishes.

Death is the end of our time here on earth and one day we will all make our transition to the afterlife. What better way to face death than to know that you did all you could to make the process of handling your transition manageable for your family? The loss of a loved one is difficult in itself. However, the situation becomes even more unbearable when someone who dies does not have their affairs in order.

As sure as we live, life happens. We hear of devastating events happening all around us. There are tragic events such as storms, earthquakes, tornadoes, floods, fires, accidents, and life-threatening illnesses. We never know if or when tragedy will strike our homes. How much more important it is to have your personal business in order? Getting your affairs in order may seem like a very grueling process. But it does not have to be, and will be worth every minute you spend in setting aside time to complete the task.

Leaving Peace and Order is about making preparations to have everything in your life in place prior to your passing. As we all know, death often gives no notification; it just shows up. Therefore, now is the time to make preparations.

This guide will walk you through the steps of gathering, recording, and storing pertinent information needed to ensure that your transition is made easy for your loved ones and to assure you the peace of mind of knowing that everything is in order.

***

CHAPTER ONE

WHY THIS GUIDE?

A few of years ago I formed a business called Ivory's Possibilities because I really enjoy helping others. I assist individuals with their personal finances through budget coaching and getting their finances and personal matters in order. As a result of talking to and listening to countless people share their personal experiences of losing loved ones, I found that many people really do not give thought to having their affairs in order until it is entirely too late. Many individuals had no idea where to locate the important papers of the loved one who recently passed away or is in the process of transitioning. They often say that the papers are probably in a drawer or box somewhere. Some individuals had expired insurance policies and/or no insurance at all. Family members were left scrambling not only to find important documents, but also scrambling and scraping up funds to bury or cremate their departed loved one. The fact that little thought or effort is given to having one's affairs in order leads to much confusion and chaos among family members when someone dies.

Another thing I discovered, during the loss of a loved one, is the family dispute over the estate, and the assumption that there was a large insurance policy, when in actuality, there was more debt left than anything else. I could go on and on with the possible horror stories resulting from someone dying and not having his or her affairs in order. However, I am sure you have stories of your own that you could share. Let us put an end to the horror stories by *Leaving Peace and Order* for our loved ones.

I encourage you to not only read this guide, but to schedule time to follow each step in completing your "Peace and Order" binder. Make it a family project. Working on this project together with your family may give you an opportunity to discuss and share your wishes with them and to hear their desires as well. This is not an easy topic to discuss and you may experience slight resistance from family members in the beginning. However, the reality of having your desires known and in writing will ensure peace in the end.

Death is not an easy subject to discuss, but it is a major part of the ultimate journey of life. Unfortunately, many people try to avoid the subject and oftentimes they feel that if they do not talk about death, it will not happen soon. Nevertheless, everyone will die; it is inevitable.

The only way one might avoid dying is to be caught up to meet the Lord, JESUS in the air! Later, I will share how you can prepare for this great event.

***

CHAPTER TWO

WHO SHOULD GET THEIR AFFAIRS IN ORDER?

If you are reading this guide, you are a prime candidate and should definitely take steps to leave your family with peace of mind in the midst of sorrow. Every adult, young or old, working, unemployed, single, married, divorced, living away from family, with or without children – should take time to get their personal affairs in order so that they can express their final wishes to their family in an organized fashion. As you take time to get your personal matters in order, you will realize the value of having this information and how important it will be to your family members handling your arrangements when you pass away.

I also encourage you to sit down with your aging parent(s) or relatives and help them get their personal estate in order. The discussion with senior citizens regarding their affairs may be difficult at first. Assure them that you are not doing this in hopes that they would die soon, but to better know and honor their final wishes.

***

CHAPTER THREE

WHAT THIS GUIDE IS NOT

This guide does not endorse any specific insurance agency, financial agency, funeral home, cemetery, or attorney. However, I will share in this guide the importance of incorporating these experts and their services to assist you in getting your affairs in place.

This guide is not a substitute for estate planning, retirement planning, financial planning, accounting services, or legal advice. Please consult an attorney, financial planner, accountant, or other licensed professional for specific questions regarding your situation.

Any results, whether good or bad, which may occur as a consequence of you taking action on any of the advice, recommendations, information or suggestions given in this guide are not the responsibility of the author.

***

CHAPTER FOUR

HOW IT ALL BEGAN

My mother's husband, Nehamas Going, passed away in 2008. His passing was a very difficult time for my mom and the family. As I watched my mom, she was extremely focused and determined to handle the affairs of her late husband. They discussed many things prior to his passing and my mom was somewhat aware of his wishes. However, some things were still left unresolved and unaccounted for; namely the property he owned. Seeing the frustration and grief my mother experienced, I decided that it was time to sit down with her to get her affairs in order.

A few years before my mother became ill, we sat down to discuss her wishes. I took the time to create a binder that housed all of her important documents. These items included insurance policies, deeds, titles, birth certificate, marriage license, social security card, financial statements, and more. I called it her "Peace and Order" binder. Additionally, my mom prepaid for much of her funeral expenses and all that remained was covered by an insurance policy specifically for her burial costs. She also gave explicit instructions on how she wanted her arrangements handled. I remember telling my best friend, Cheryl, that I had to take off my daughter hat and put on my professional organizer hat while discussing and handling my mother's affairs. This talk with my mom was not easy or normal, especially when I was expecting her to live a long life. Nevertheless, the discussion was not only important but necessary. As a result of our conversation, my mom's final wishes were very clear to me.

My Mom's Story...

In September 2005 my mom, after being diagnosed with breast cancer had a mastectomy on her right breast. She believed that God was going to bring her through the surgery and He did! During this time, mom refused chemotherapy and radiation treatments. She worked in the healthcare arena for many years and saw the effects of these treatments on others; two of which were her own mother and one of her sisters. Thankfully, the cancer did not spread and she was cancer free for seven years.

Later, my mom developed other medical issues. She had high blood pressure for many years and was a borderline diabetic. These diseases along with the medication she was taking affected her heart and kidneys. Even through these health challenges, my mom stood firm on the Word of

God: "By Jesus' stripes I am healed!" God had proven Himself faithful to her during the time of the breast cancer and she was trusting that His will would continue to be done in her life. Mom shared her testimony of how God spared her from the ill effects of cancer and of His goodness to her. She testified to anyone who would listen. She especially shared her testimony with the doctors and nurses who cared for her. They often said my mom was a very peculiar woman. Mom just believed God's Word!

My mom's parents died in their early to mid-sixties and many of mom's siblings passed away at young ages. She consequently did not think that she would live to see the age of 70; the promised age mentioned in the Bible. I remember a few months before my mom's 70th birthday that she became very ill and ended up in the hospital. It was in the back of my mind, and I am sure hers, as to whether she was going to pull through. *(Be careful of the thoughts and words you entertain.)* Nevertheless, God was gracious to my mother. She not only lived to see her 70th birthday, but on February 15, 2012, she celebrated her 71st birthday as well.

It was October 2012 when my mom became ill again. We took her to the hospital where she was admitted. She was literally in the hospital for 20 days before passing. Mom was adamant about not going through dialysis. However, after being in the hospital a few days, the doctor persuaded her that having the treatments was in her best interest. Agreeing, mom had dialysis treatments two days in a row. Unfortunately, after the second dialysis treatment, the very next morning mom had a stroke and ended up in ICU. I watched my mom's health deteriorate in literally 20 days. Yet, I saw her faith, strength and courage throughout the entire ordeal. When she finally gave up her fight to live, I watched her peacefully slip from time to eternity.

On the morning that my mom passed away, I woke up very early and went into our prayer room before 6:00 a.m. I began to cry out to the Lord. My prayer was, "Not my will Lord, but Thy will be done." As I was praying, a song came to mind. It was called *Praise You In This Storm* by Casting Crowns. I found the song on YouTube and played it over and over again as I worshipped and cried before the Lord. I even posted the link to the song on my Facebook page. I made up my mind that I was going to do what my Pastor, Kimberly Ray Gavin, often says, "Accept what God allows." I began to Praise the Lord in my storm.

After an hour or so, I went back to bed and fell asleep. When I awakened, it was after 9:00 a.m. I jumped up, with a sense of urgency, showered and dressed up a bit. *I knew The Lord was going to take my mom that day.* My husband was surprised that I was leaving so suddenly. I told him to come on later.

When I got to the hospital, my mom was awake. I sat with her, but she did not say anything. I took out my phone and found a scripture in the Bible and read it to her. Tearfully, I read, *"For I am now ready to be offered, and the time of my departure is at hand. I have fought a good fight, I have finished my course, I have kept the faith: Henceforth there is laid up for me a crown of righteousness, which the Lord, the righteous judge, shall give me at that day: and not to me only, but unto all them also that love his appearing."* (2 Timothy 4:6-8 KJV)

When I finished reading, with tears in my eyes, I said, "Mom, I release you - me, Amy, AmBree, Chappy and Douglas will be alright. You may go to be with JESUS." My mom sighed, as if relieved, and turned her head. I moved away from her bed and I peacefully waited. Forty minutes or so later my mom was gone.

When my mom took her final breath, the head nurse pronounced her dead at 10:55 a.m. I looked up to the heavens and said, "Thank you Lord - I Praise YOU!" The nurses were amazed at my serenity. But I knew it was *"the peace of God which passeth all understanding."*

My mother passed away on October 28, 2012, at the age of 71, due to kidney failure and congestive heart failure. Yes, I grieved the loss of my dear mother, but, I did not go through the stress or drama that some families experience when their loved one's affairs are not in order. My mom was adamant about what she wanted; I obeyed and was able to handle her arrangements with ease.

One thing I can truly say, after the passing of my mother, is that God gave me supernatural peace! I had the peace of knowing that my mom's affairs were in order and that I was honoring her wishes to the letter.

"And the peace of God, which passeth all understanding, shall keep your hearts and minds through Christ Jesus." – Philippians 4:7 (KJV)

~~~

I realize that this topic may seem a bit morbid. Yet, think of the peace of mind you and your family will have knowing that your affairs are in order. Every family deserves that assurance, and the best way for them to have it is for you to get your personal matters organized. This guide, **Leaving Peace and Order**, will help you accomplish just that.

***

CHAPTER FIVE

EXPERIENCES OF FAMILY AND FRIENDS

As I was working on this project, many personal situations of family and friends came to mind. I polled a few and requested that they candidly share their experiences of losing a loved one and on handling the arrangements. I asked them the following questions: What would be the one thing they wished they or their loved one had done? What problem, if any, did they face? And, what advice would they give to those planning to get their affairs in order now?

I would like to share with you a selection of real events. Each case is unique, but carries the same message of the importance of getting your affairs in order so you can *Leave Peace and Order* for your family. *(I chose to remove all names to respect the privacy of each family.)*

CASE #1: On September 10, 1998, a healthy 33 year old daughter was tragically killed in an automobile accident. Her father shares:

No one ever wants to experience the death of a child, regardless of their age. Losing our daughter was the most devastating experience my wife and I could ever have. Although it has been almost sixteen years, it is still very difficult to talk about the accident. Our daughter was a lovely young woman. She was vibrant. She loved life and her family. But most importantly, she loved her Savior, Jesus

Christ. It was through her death that my wife and I came to know Christ in a real way.

My wife and I had only one child. We loved her dearly. She was killed in a single car accident. It was a freak accident and we are still baffled by how it happened. She was on her way to work and never made it.

Our daughter was very independent. She had life insurance through her employer. However, we also had a life insurance policy for her, since she was a child. Therefore, I had no problems in making and paying for her funeral arrangements.

The one thing that I would recommend, besides insuring your children, is that they give someone trustworthy access to their bank account and assign beneficiaries to their accounts. The process that an individual has to go through to manage the affairs of a deceased loved one can be very daunting and often may require legal intervention. Therefore, make sure adequate life insurance is in place for both you and your children, and that legal documentation or property assignments are given. When you take these steps, you will be **Leaving Peace and Order** *for your family.*

~~~

CASE #2: **On April 16, 1997, a healthy 40 year old husband and father of three daughters, was tragically killed in a motorcycle accident. His wife shares:**

My husband was a healthy strong man. He was a devoted husband and loving father. We were enjoying life in serving the Lord with our three daughters. It was on a Sunday morning when my husband rode his motorcycle to go clean the church before morning services. When he was returning home to get dressed for church, he was struck by a drunk driver. He died of internal bleeding. Needless to say, I was devastated. I truly thank GOD for His love and strength which carried me through that life-altering event.

My husband and I were relatively young. We had not discussed death much other than my husband insisting that I DO NOT spend a lot of money on caskets. We had most of our important papers (like house deeds, car titles, birth certificates, insurance papers) in a lock box, so finding most of our documents was not too hard. But to say that I understood what was covered in our medical and life insurance policies was an understatement. I was a little more familiar with the coverage I had through my employer, but I had no idea what kind of coverage for medical or life insurance my husband had through his job. Sad to say, I knew we were covered, but that was about it.

I did not know what funerals, grave sites or tomb stones cost. My husband's job, a day or two after he passed, sent me a check for $2,500 to cover funeral costs which they later deducted from his final paycheck, vacation pay, etc. However, GOD was so good; He really saw me through every step.

My brother-in-law and a brother from my church both worked closely with me. If items were missing like medical benefits, they would ask about it and I would search for them in another box in my room with those items in it. They went through all of our papers, polices, (including bills) and wrote down for me what each policy covered, balances and what I needed to do to get things transferred over to my name, etc. They even tallied up our debt. Because the brother from my church worked for Allstate at the time, he requested a rush on issuing the life insurance payout and literally put together a binder outlining what steps I needed to take next. I was so truly grateful for all their help; however, I did somewhat feel invaded. If my husband and I had our records more organized, I could have just handed my information to whoever was helping me and not have to search for items or say, "I don't know", concerning policies. Or, I could have even handled some issues myself because I would have been informed.

I received so much help initially, but later on I think if I just knew what to do, other than continue to pay my bills, it would have helped me tremendously. I had so many decisions to make. My husband had retirement funds that I could cash (and pay a penalty) or roll over into another retirement account. I had two cars. Should I sell one? Should I pay the house off entirely or just make payments until the mortgage is paid in full? Should I put money into an IRA account (what is an IRA?) I really could have used help with these types of questions and concerns. I certainly wanted to have godly wisdom because my children were relatively young, so not only my future, but their needs were a huge concern to me.

*My final thought and advice would be that even though you may hate to discuss death and funeral arrangements, etc. it is so important to do so. I guess when I was younger, I thought about folks dying in their 80s and 90s but so many are dying so much younger, so it is best to be prepared. I encourage you to follow the directives in this guide, **Leaving Peace and Order**, and create a binder that contains all of your medical, dental, auto and life insurance policies. Review your policies periodically and perhaps highlight or type what each policy covers so that you are well aware of what they contain. Have a list of your creditors and their* *contact information. Take time to list out your retirement accounts and numbers. Make sure your loved ones have access to all bank account numbers or funds. Write down your wishes for funeral arrangements and even try to have the funeral expenses paid off in advance, if possible. Make a will if you have monies or property that you want to leave to others. The less your family has to be concerned with or have to figure out the better.*

~~~

CASE #3: On March 1999, a healthy 43 year old husband and father died. His wife shares:

My husband was a healthy and strong young man. He was very fit with no fat on his body at all. He smoked (Kool) cigarettes since he was 17 years old. He said his father told him if you can afford to buy them you can smoke them; always be able to support your own habit.

27

One day we were getting ready to go to the circus in Chicago, my husband said this would be the last time we take our daughter there because she was getting too old for the circus. So, I drove there and he was to drive back; that is just how we shared driving. On the way back to the car he asked me to drive, he said he was not feeling well and that I needed to drive. I said no you just do not want to drive. Then my daughter said, "Mom, you better drive dad is staggering."

I started driving home and by the time I made it out of the city, my husband was in the passenger seat in a fetal position. Now, this was very unusual for him because he had a high tolerance for pain. While I was praying and asking God what to do, my husband was telling me to take him home. I continued to pray, Lord, I need to hear from you, this is unusual for him. I remember asking my husband a week before about the Tylenol pain reliever he had taken. I noticed that the bottle of 500 pills was almost empty. I asked him if he had been taking all of those pills and he responded yes, he had a headache he could not get rid of. I told him he should have told me earlier and that it was not good to take so many pills. So, while I was praying, the entire incident came back to my remembrance. I heard the Lord clearly say to me to take him to the hospital; they will find something in his head. THEY DID.

My healthy husband was lying in the emergency room in severe pain. My daughter and her friend were in the waiting room. I did not know what to think or what to do. I just prayed and prayed. I got myself together to call the parents of the little girl who went to the circus with my daughter. They came to the hospital to pick up their daughter as well as my daughter.

The doctors ran several tests on my husband, and yes they found a mass in his head, which they called a brain lesion. I did not care for the name lesion; God knows I did not want to hear any of that. The doctors kept my husband in the hospital for over two to three weeks for tests, biopsies and more testing. The final diagnosis was that my husband had lung and brain cancer. We were shocked! We had to start thinking about the impossible and the "what if" and "what of" and "how do you want to go", if the inevitable happened.

Let me tell you this, when my husband was diagnosed with cancer, we only had the life insurance policy from my job and we were able to get a burial policy that same month he was diagnosed all by the blessing of the Lord. God had given us great favor.

The time passed by so quickly. There were doctor appointments, hospital visits and a great amount of stress to my heart. Although we did not want to talk about arrangements, we had to and we did. I asked my husband what color suit, casket and flower arrangement he wanted and the time and the place? He did not belong to a church, however, he was saved. I asked who would he like to preach his eulogy, and did he want his wedding ring and glasses on or off? We talked about it all; the only thing was we did not discuss his insurance policy. I was so distraught that I totally forgot to discuss his insurance. When I went to make arrangements, I was so out of it, I told the funeral director that my husband did not have any insurance, although later, I found out that he did.

*If I would have had **Leaving Peace and Order** I would have only needed to pick up my binder and I would have had all our information at hand.*

*It was not all that bad, the insurance agent did everything for me and I was able to bury my husband without any problems. **Leaving Peace and Order** is very important.*

My husband was 43 years of age and I was 39 when God took him home.

~~~

CASE #4: On October 29, 1997, a 49 year old mother passed away due to a heart attack, and February 2006 a father died of lung cancer. Their daughter shares:

Losing a loved one is one of the most difficult times you will face in your life. Having lost both parents has been very challenging, as my mom passed when I was 23 years old. I have two younger brothers, and at the time they were 15 and 16 and in High School. When my mom passed away at the age of 49, she was uninsured which added to the stress of losing her. My mom had some health issues that are still undefined to this day. All I remember about my mother's health problems was that she was on a lot of medications which I believe resulted in her heart attack. Since my mom had no life insurance, I bore the responsibility of having to plan a funeral with very little money. I had to rely on family and friends to assist monetarily. Fortunately, I come from a close-knit family, so they stepped up and helped plan a beautiful home-going service for my mother.

One thing I learned after experiencing the loss of my mother was how important it is to have life insurance to help pay for funeral expenses. Having life insurance in place will make losing a loved one a lot less stressful, as funeral costs can be very expensive and financial stress is one of the worst stresses a person can experience. After my mom's untimely death, I made sure to have life insurance policies in place for my dad and brothers.

In February 2006, my dad died from lung cancer. He battled lung cancer for many years. When my dad passed, it was not as devastating as losing my mom, because I was more prepared. I had purchased a small life insurance policy years prior to his death which I was able to use at his time of death.

If you will be responsible for a family member at their time of death, I greatly urge you to make sure you are aware of their health and state of well-being. Also, it is very important to know what their financial affairs are prior to their death. Then, you are able to help them make the decision about purchasing an adequate amount of life insurance.

*The guidelines in **Leaving Peace and Order** will help you eliminate the stress of trying to figure out what you should do in the event a loved one passes away and does not have life insurance or enough money for proper funeral arrangements.*

~~~

CASE #5: **On January 23, 2003, a 57 year old husband, father, and Pastor unexpectedly died of congestive heart failure. His daughter shares:**

My father was a healthy active 57 year old. One day he went to the doctor because he was having difficulty breathing. He was informed that he had fluid on his lungs and was diagnosed with congestive heart failure. The doctors said if he ever had problems with his heart failing he would not survive because his heart was too weak. The diagnosis and his passing occurred within a year.

In December 2002 my dad asked me to be the mistress of ceremony at his church for his birthday celebration. When I agreed, I never imagined it would turn out almost to be a celebration of me. My dad would not allow us to celebrate him; the entire service consisted of my dad celebrating my life as a wife, mother and Christian. Later that month, he asked that our family spend Christmas together in Wisconsin Dells. We never took a trip together like that before. I remember my mother preparing Christmas dinner and taking it to the Dells. Although this was strange to us, we complied with my father's wishes as this was his desire, and we wanted to honor his request. We wanted him to be happy as he was getting weaker and was not very mobile at the time. I had no idea he was rapidly deteriorating and would soon die. The vacation at the Dells was the last time we were all together as a family.

The morning of his passing my mother told me she took my dad to the hospital because he said he was having problems breathing. In the car, all the way to the hospital, he sang the song "Thank You Lord for all You've Done for Me." When they arrived at the hospital my mom said they were in a room waiting to be seen by the doctor and my dad said he could not breathe. He gasped, closed his eyes, and passed away.

My father passed away in January and I remember that day as though it were yesterday. I was in a meeting at work with a gentleman who was trying to sell me school encyclopedias. My office phone rang during the meeting, it was my mother crying. She was telling me I needed to come to Chicago immediately because my dad was in the hospital. I was in Wisconsin at the time. I was thinking how do I get from Wisconsin to Chicago immediately. I ended the meeting and grabbed my coat. I received another call before I left work but this time it was from my dad's secretary who was with my dad and mom at the hospital. She wanted to make sure I was on my way. While she was speaking I heard a scream and a machine beeping and the phone went dead. I ran out the office over to my cousin's office to tell her what was happening. She immediately got on the phone to call the hospital to see what was going on. My cousin was told my dad had passed away. That day changed my life!

I was now on a journey of planning a funeral. I am an only child and my father did not leave a will or instructions concerning his affairs. My father was a Pastor and a high ranking Mason. Both groups had their own ideas of how my father should be celebrated and buried. Trying to make arrangements with everyone giving their opinions on where my father's funeral should take place, who should officiate, and how the service should be organized was overwhelming. If my dad had left instructions outlining his desires, it would have saved my mom and me a great deal of pain in planning while at the same time grieving his sudden departure. I believe having your affairs in order will save loved ones time, undo pressure and stress during the grieving process.

My recommendations to Pastors are 1) Have a succession plan in place. My father did not have an Assistant Pastor. Make sure there are bylaws and the bylaws address the untimely passing of the Pastor. 2) Make sure it is clear who from the church will be responsible for working with the family (i.e., planning of funeral) if family needs assistance. **Leaving Peace and Order** *will assist you in following my recommendations.*

~~~

CASE #6: **On May 29, 2002, a 59 year old father passed away due to End Stage Congestive Heart Failure. His daughter shares:**

My father was only 59 years old, yet his health was failing. He needed to have a heart transplant. Unfortunately, because of his lifestyle he was denied being placed on the transplant recipient's list. He refused to change his lifestyle and did not follow the doctor's recommendations to add years to his life. He only received medical care when the illness caused him to be hospitalized. He later died while an inpatient in the hospital.

My dad had no preparations and I did not know what to do. I followed the lead of family members and funeral home staff. Things as simple as clothes and hair were baffling to me. I knew my dad wore braids, so I had the funeral staff braid his hair. One of the funeral directors provided the clothing for my dad. I was floored when I was made aware of the prices. My cousin/his niece paid for the majority of the funeral costs. (I don't know what would have happened had she not stepped in.) My younger brother contributed $200. I wish my dad at least had a small insurance policy; just enough to take care of his funeral expenses.

I was a young single mother with two boys. I was working at a nursing home during that time. I really did not have a lot of money. I can remember looking at the funeral costs, and realized burial was not an option. So I *chose cremation. This was not an option that I wanted; however, this was the option that was most affordable. When I look back, it is horrible to make a final decision based on lack of funds. I personally believe that each decision making process in the final stages of one's life should be well planned. The funeral home services did not include the cremation vase; therefore, I had the funeral home hold my father's cremains until I was able to afford an urn. The funeral director knew my situation and worked with me. At the end of it all, I had to pay approximately $1,400 out-of-pocket.*

Given the example of my father's situation, I would encourage everyone to get some type of life insurance, or put some money away for burial arrangements. As I recall, I do not think I ever got a chance to grieve. I was too busy piecing things together. And, that is how

I felt, "I pieced my dad's funeral together!" Insurance policies are actually quite affordable. My mom's life insurance is through AARP. I have a policy for myself, my husband and kids. I have come to know it is not about the money you will get when a loved one passes; it is about taking care of the loved one's final resting place. I used to think life insurance was about leaving others money – no, please understand, life insurance is about planning for "your final resting place." It is a hard conversation to have and we all try to stay away from it. However, it is much needed – **Leaving Peace and Order** *can help you have that conversation with your family.*

I can also remember dealing with Social Security for my dad; I did not know a lot of information. I was again thankful, that the people at the Social Security office worked with me. I was guided step-by-step on what to do and how to do it. I am currently up to date on all my mom's affairs such as medical, financial, funeral planning (she wants to be cremated like her spouse).

Lastly, I will say, because of the issues with my dad, when my mom's husband died in 2008, I knew what to do. I allowed my mom to grieve as I planned his final resting place. Handling his affairs was much easier; he did have life insurance and this allowed things to be less of a hassle. My mom knew her husband wanted to be cremated and the funeral home arranged the services at a veteran's cemetery with a 21-gun salute with the military. I have been on both ends of the spectrum; I see how just a few minutes of planning can mean a world of difference. Please, take the time to use this guide,

Leaving Peace and Order, to make the proper plans.

~~~

CASE #7: **On May 19, 2013, due to cancer, a prominent woman in the educational field, in her early 60s unexpectedly passed away. Her co-worker shares:**

I remember when my supervisor passed away and how overwhelmed we all were at the office. My supervisor was a prominent Educational Leader who made a significant impact in the lives of children throughout the city. Death within itself is overwhelming, but because her death was sudden and unexpected it was even harder to handle. She and I worked together for over 15 years, so we developed a relationship that went beyond that of employee and employer, to that of friends. We watched each other's children grow up and we became an emotional strength to one another naturally and spiritually.

My supervisor's death occurred within a two week period. I remember looking at her one day and asking what was going on with her, and she replied, "Why do you ask?" She told me she was not feeling well and thought it may have been something she ate. The next day she did not come to work. I immediately became concerned because she worked 12-hour days and weekends and never missed work. I called to check on her but she did not answer the phone. Two days passed and I still had not heard from her so I called her daughter. Her daughter informed me her mom was okay but was taking some time off because she was not feeling well. A few days later I received a call from my supervisor and her daughter stating my supervisor had cancer. Within a week of receiving that news she passed away.

I was now the person responsible for communicating this information to students, staff, parents, and the community. As a small school, we did not have a protocol in place for dealing with situations of this magnitude. My colleagues and I were responsible for fielding communication of her death to the news and other public relations groups.

What I found to be most challenging during this time was trying to close out the school year without our leader. I had not anticipated the challenges that were in store as we moved to close out the year. My supervisor had a brilliant way of thinking and was very intellectual. She stored passwords, dates, and important information in her head. Because she was this type of thinker it made it difficult for me to pick up where she left off. We found ourselves searching for log-ins, passwords, and documents to no avail. This meant we had to start over by recreating documents which became a tedious experience along with dealing with her passing.

I learned several valuable lessons going through this experience. I first learned the significance of writing everything down (i.e., passwords, dates, etc.) and putting them in a place accessible to others. The second lesson I learned was to make sure I am not the only person holding information and important documentation. I now ensure that there are multiple copies of files and that they are kept in a location where others can find them.

Leaving Peace and Order *is not only beneficial to family members, but going through the organizing process can be helpful to your employer, especially if it is a small company or private organization.*

~~~

<u>CASE #8:</u> On October 30, 2012, a 65 year old husband passed away due to a heart attack. His wife shares:

My husband of 44 years had always been the backbone of our marriage and family. He lost his father when he was only nine years old. That loss made a heavy impact on his life and ultimately when we met, fell in love, and had our two children, he devoted his life to us.

My husband suffered from high blood pressure, heart disease and diabetes. He also suffered from multiple back surgeries which escalated his diabetes due to his inability to walk freely. Eventually the diabetes impacted his vision. Through all of these issues his positive attitude was amazing. He always looked on the bright side and kept us looking forward.

We had just returned from a wonderful week's vacation in his beloved northland - ironically talking about me retiring, and we were looking forward to our future. I came home from work on Tuesday evening. My husband had prepared a home-made meal of sauerkraut and ribs and we enjoyed our meal and conversation. We received a call from one of our grandchildren asking us to help him with a confirmation class assignment prior to his first communion, that led to a deep conversation of trust and putting your life in God's hands. My husband told me that very evening that he felt strongly that God was with him and that Jesus was his Savior.

We then turned on the TV to watch a show we were looking forward to seeing – we were really enjoying it - actually laughing out loud. I was sitting on the couch and my husband on his recliner kind of to the side of me. I heard this strange noise and turned to him. I thought he was teasing me as it was Halloween eve, and he was such a jokester. Only to realize he was in distress; I immediately called 911.

Within two hours my husband was called to be with his Lord.

All of this happened so quickly, I did not know where to turn, what to do next. How would I know what to do without my soul-mate? I was given the name of a local funeral home to make arrangements to have my husband's remains transported from Illinois to Wisconsin. I called that evening and made an appointment for the next day. I was in a daze. Thank goodness for my family! The next morning I made a call to the funeral home in Wisconsin where he would be buried and they arranged everything.

Following the funeral service for my husband, I had to return to Illinois to an empty house, his empty recliner and re-live those last moments of his life. My rock was gone and I felt so isolated and alone. I did not have a plan or direction. I just drove to church. When I arrived, my pastor was there and we talked and shared the grief of losing a loved one. We prayed and I felt close to God, like He was there with me, guiding me.

The night my husband died, I received an unexpected call in the middle of the night from someone who wanted to harvest his eyes. After much pressure from the caller I responded absolutely not! The next morning I was told the hospital would not release my husband's body as they were harvesting his organs. Thanks to my Wisconsin funeral director, who was able to intervene for me, my husband's body was not compromised. It seems death turns into a business for some, without any compassion for the family, and when you are not thinking clearly, you need someone you can trust to protect you. While at the hospital you are handed papers and told you need to sign; you are numb and cannot even comprehend what has just happened; much less understand what all is being said to you.

Although my husband had health issues, we did not discuss the "what ifs". I think we both felt if we discussed it, we were giving in to the inevitable and we had so many hopes and dreams for our future. I am so grateful for the help and support of my funeral director who guided me through all the papers and processes that needed to be completed. He also is a financial advisor; so needless to say, he has been able to put my affairs in order. He guided me through the maze of issues (medical insurance, deeds, wills, living estates, life insurance, powers of attorney for healthcare and financials, Social Security, etc.) Some of which I did not even know needed to be addressed. Without his support I would not have known what to do. But thanks to him, when I pass, my children will only have to make one call and my affairs have all been organized for them.

There have been numerous wonderments over this past year. I know I could not have survived without God's grace and intervention. I feel there were times when my strength was so fragile I could not bear to wake up in the morning, only to awake to a bright sun and a beautiful cardinal on my deck; my husband's favorite bird. Or, a moose sighted in an area where they had never been seen before; in a favorite place of my husband's. I cannot explain these events, but I know I have been blessed and I feel very close to God. The pain of losing my spouse of 44 years is incomprehensible, but with God to guide me through whatever He has in his great plan, I can do it. I know we'll be together again and all my "whys" will be answered.

*I wish I would have had **"Leaving Peace and Order"** at a time when my husband and I could have gone through it together. I think I made wise choices - choices that my husband would have wanted. But, I can only pray I acted in accordance with his wishes. I do know, after my passing, my children will be in a better position to deal with all of the final arrangements that need to be handled. My children will both receive a copy of this book.*

I know God is with me.

~~~

CASE #9: **On June 2, 2010, a 68 year old woman passed away from lung cancer. Her daughter shares:**

My mom appeared to me to be the epitome of health. I had no idea my mother was ill. Often when I would speak to her on the phone, however, I noticed an increase in coughing spells. Concerned, I would ask her about the coughing spells and she would casually brush it off. Later, I found out that my mom was coughing up blood.

Two weeks before my mother passed away, my siblings and I found out that she had lung cancer. We were devastated! We wondered how long our mother had known she was ill and had not told us. The timing was difficult to process. Her health deteriorated so swiftly. We did not realize our mother would be gone so quickly.

Fortunately, when my mom passed away, we were relieved to find that my mom had made some preparations and her burial arrangements were paid in full. The issue we ran into, however, was the transferring of my mom's property. I believe if she had me and/or one of my siblings' names on her mortgage, it would have been a bit easier to handle the process of transferring her property. The challenge was that four of her five children did not live in the same state she lived in. So it would have made sense if my mom had placed my sister's name on her mortgage, since she lived in the same state as my mom; this would have made the handling of mom's property a lot smoother.

The advice I would offer is to be sure you talk to your family members/loved ones and share with them any and all health issues you are experiencing. No one wants to find out that a loved one is dying of cancer or any disease, two weeks before that loved one dies. Please, please, please do not keep your failing health a secret from your loved ones in hopes of protecting them from worrying about you. It is far more devastating to not have known and then find out when it is too late.

Another recommendation is to make sure that you complete the proper legal documentations to ensure that your property can be transferred to the person of choice. These documents may include a quit claim deed, a will or trust.

I would also advise that you discuss with your family your final wishes and put them in writing. If you are involved in a church or ministry, make sure your family knows the role in which you would like your church/ministry to play. Document your requests and make sure not only your family has a copy, but your church/ministry has a copy in their files for you.

*Finally, be sure your family is aware of where you keep your insurance policies and important documents. **Leaving Peace and Order** will assist you in making the appropriate preparations.*

~~~

CASE #10: **On February 10, 2007, a 69 year old mother unexpectedly dies of a massive heart attack. Her daughter shares:**

My mother was mobile and in fair health. The morning of her death I had coffee with her, we laughed and talked. I always kissed her on her forehead when I left her house. I remember kissing her that day. I visited my mother daily and had no clue I was going to lose her. Nothing indicated she was sick.

My mother had a massive heart attack in a Verizon Phone Store; she just collapsed and nobody knew CPR. By the time the ambulance arrived and I actually made it to the store - reality kicked me in my face!!!! When we made it to the hospital, she was already brain-dead.

The decision not to keep her on a ventilator had to be made. Although my mother left a folder/envelope with her burial wishes, it did not include the decision to keep her alive on a machine or not. We assumed as a family that she did not want to live this way. Of course, one family member did not agree. It created such a rash of negative events, family arguing, grandchildren having to see such madness, distress all over everyone and then the final - we had to "pull the plug". I was devastated - not because of the decision, but, due to the reality my mother was no longer alive.

*Since the insurance and other details were in the envelope, the **one decision we had to make almost destroyed us as a family**. My mother always instilled in us the importance of family. We did not have any other problems because of the "famous" envelope - but that one missing detail resulted in no peace. I was miserable throughout the entire process and several months later because of the negative memory. If there was nothing documented or no envelope, I cannot imagine how **Peace and Order** would comfort my family.*

*My personal advice is to take the time to sit down with your family and work on **"Leaving Peace and Order"**. Prepare a living will, which includes a "Do Not Resuscitate" (DNR) order, if that is your choice. Have the information documented so it is readily available. It will save you and your family unnecessary distress.*

~~~

CASE #11: On December 4, 2008, due to congestive heart failure, an 81 year old father passes away. His daughter shares:

My father was a very energetic man. He was also a very caring and loving father. My father's health deteriorated as he aged, yet he was a fighter to the end.

One of my main wishes was that my father had a will and I knew where he kept it. A will would have made the handling of his estate much easier.

I am thankful, however, that my name was not on the deed for his house. There were issues concerning one of my brothers as it relates to my dad's house, and I knew if my name was on the deed, it would have been a disaster. Therefore, as the eldest daughter handling my father's affairs, I decided to let the mortgage company take the house — a true blessing in disguise.

Given that my dad's house was not paid for upon his passing, I wish he had secured a reverse mortgage. A reverse mortgage would have eliminated my dad from having to make mortgage payments in his ailing years.

When dealing with older parents or family members who are of the old mindset — thinking they don't need insurance, I would advise that you try to explain to them the importance of having insurance, or at least setting aside enough money to cover their burial expenses. This might be difficult, but do the best you can in encouraging your loved one.

Daddy saved what he needed to be buried and we had no problem. However, some people might think, 'but he did not leave any for you all' and my answer to that is it really does not matter, he left enough.

*Likewise, make sure everything is where it should be as far as important papers, birth certificates, insurance papers, mortgage papers and Do Not Resuscitate (DNR) paperwork. If you follow the steps in this guide, you can **Leave Peace and Order** for your family.*

~~~

CASE #12: On April 30, 2010, due to congestive heart failure, an 88 year old man made his transition. His stepdaughter shares:

My dad was pretty organized and had all his financial papers, bills, and medical benefits in a couple of places, so we did not have to look everywhere for information. He also was sort of a history buff; he had a book that he created with a history of things he and his family had done. I would say this was the most helpful in making the obituary for the funeral service. Oftentimes you know of the history you have with someone while living with them, but there may be so many more details of their life that you may want to incorporate into the obituary that you do not know. My dad was an only child and was preceded in death by all of the older relatives who would have been able to give us a little history of his younger days. The scrapbook he had of his life was invaluable to us. I certainly wish we had looked at it earlier with him and talked about some of his accomplishments more.

My mom and stepdad conducted their financial affairs completely separately. My dad handled some bills and my mom handled others. Thank GOD, my dad had most of his financial documents, bills, medical insurance papers, etc. in one place so we did not have to search through much. My dad was wheelchair bound. Therefore, my mom handled his banking for him and had her name on his account so she could administer his affairs. Also, due to my dad's failing health, my mom pressed my dad within months of his passing about funeral wishes. Other than attempting to summarize my dad's life for the obituary, we did not run into too many problems. I had to really pore over insurance/medical papers and explain to my mom what needed to be done to continue or cancel coverage, and write down numbers that needed to be called, and requirements needed.

Even though you may not care to discuss the subject of death now, it is much better for the family members (who are in the midst of grief) to know what the deceased desires regarding funeral arrangements, money *matters, etc., and have all the documents in one place and in order. To have to search though old letters and documents trying to find insurance policies numbers, mortgage deeds, car titles, bill accounts, etc. can be daunting. Even when you have searched through everything, you are still left wondering if there is something out there you may have missed or know nothing about.*

*Love that title of **Leaving Peace and Order!** If you **do** have your documents in order and your policies are understood by loved ones, you will have great peace even before the Lord calls you home and your loved ones will have peace that all has been addressed and is in order.*

~~~

CASE #13: **On July 22, 2012, a grandmother of 94 years of age chooses to depart this life on earth. Her granddaughter shares:**

My grandmother was generally a healthy individual throughout her entire life with only a couple of minor surgeries due to birthing 13 children. She was never hospitalized for severe illness or disease until she reached her 90s.

Grandma's death was a complete shock to her entire enormous family, but inevitable considering her age.

We celebrated my grandmother's 94th birthday in April 2012. Subsequently her health deteriorated rapidly. After many, many trips to the doctor's office and many hospitalizations, we were bewildered and beyond stressed as the harsh reality of death drew nigh.

My grandmother started to develop extreme stomach discomfort and eating had become a task for her. The doctors suspected colon cancer, but since she had no desire to be sedated and endure a colonoscopy, she gave up on her will to live on July 22, 2012 with me by her side.

After death came the daunting task for her most responsible daughter to distribute the inheritance monies. For the most part, dividing the monetary allowance was not an issue. Grandma made her funeral wishes known to her two most trusted daughters.

One of the daughters endured ridicule and there was bickering amongst the siblings in regards to how much money they each received. There was no will or trust, only an insurance policy and lifelong savings, which left some to wonder if they received their "fair" share. Initially, no one really had any idea how much money was available, and when it came to dividing personal items within grandmother's home, there were minor verbal disagreements over living room furniture and clothing items, and the coveted family photos that had been in the family for decades. The confusion and wonderment of what items belonged to what individuals could have been avoided if legal documentation was in place.

I recommend that all families legally create and update their documented wishes and have wills, trusts, advanced directives, etc. in place. Also, in a perfect world, large and small families should at least have meetings on how they will handle the inevitability of dealing with elderly parents. Having these meetings will help to ensure that everyone knows where each stands, and will alleviate as much stress as possible. Death is never easy, but everyone *should take comfort in knowing that their "affairs are in order" – thus **Leaving Peace and Order** for their families!!!*

~~~

As you have read from the various cases, it is evident that we have no control over death and that death is not deterred by one's age. However, we can take control over our affairs and make sure that we take the steps to **Leave Peace and Order** for our family and loved ones by following the directives in this guide. As you can see in each case, if loved ones would have taken the time to discuss and document their final wishes, shared information about their health, reviewed and understood their medical and life insurance policies, created a will or trust, stated what role their church/ministry was to play, and many of the steps mentioned in this guide, some of the stress of handling their loved one's passing would have been eliminated.

Keep reading...this guide will make you think and it will help you get your affairs in order.

CHAPTER SIX

ESTATE PLANNING

As I stated, the purpose of this guide is to encourage you to make your final wishes known to your family/loved ones and to direct you step-by-step in gathering, recording, and storing your important information and documents. However, I would like to also stress the importance of estate planning. Estate planning enables you to make the decision today of how and to whom you want your assets distributed once you die. Estate planning may involve you contacting a financial advisor to help you get your financial affairs in order; and securing an attorney who will assist you in legally getting your estate affairs in order and the proper documents in place, which may include a will, trust, living trust, etc.

You may say, I am not wealthy, I do not have much; but let me assure you that everything you have is considered your estate. Your estate or assets includes your checking and savings accounts, auto, home, other property, furniture, investments, life insurance, and all of your personal belongings. No matter how small or large your estate may be, you have one and you cannot take it with you when you die. Someone will get it and you have the opportunity now to designate who should take ownership by making preparations through estate planning.

You may also elect to leave a certain amount of money or certain items to the charitable organization of your choice; you have the opportunity of making this request through estate planning.

Estate planning not only involves who will receive your assets when you are gone; but estate planning begins with you building wealth, getting out of debt, having the proper insurance in place, and so much more. You have the chance to enjoy your estate, now, and bless your family/loved ones and favorite charitable organization when you pass away.

Estate planning includes some of the the following components:

- Will - a legal document stating who should receive your assets after you pass away. It also allows you to designate who should be the legal guardian of your child(ren).

- Trust - a legal instrument allowing you to set conditions on how and when your assets are to be distributed without having to go through probate court, thus reducing delay; minimizing gift and estate taxes; and allowing you to be very decisive in your distributions.

- Powers of Attorney - documents giving an individual the legal right to act on your behalf when you are unable to do so yourself. This includes handling your personal business affairs (power of attorney for property) and make medical decision for you (healthcare power of attorney).

- A Living Will – a legal document stating your desire to withdraw from sustainability in the event you become permanently unconscious or terminally ill with no hopes of recovering. This is where you state the "Do Not Resuscitate – DNR" order.

Estate planning is so important today. I encourage you to sit down with a financial advisor and/or an attorney to get your affairs in order. However, in the meantime, please follow the steps in this guide to begin the process. You will be well on your way by the time you meet with a financial planner and/or attorney, because you will have the majority of your information in order. Doing so will allow you to *Leave Peace and Order* for your family and loved ones.

CHAPTER SEVEN

WHAT ARE YOUR FINAL WISHES?

Before you gather your information, take time to think about what you desire as your final wishes. Then think of the preparations made for someone close to you. Think of the order or lack of order there was in making the arrangements for that individual. You have the opportunity now to be very specific with your requests. If the person you select is trustworthy, you can have peace of mind knowing that your desires will be honored and that you are *Leaving Peace and Order* for your family - a very special gift!

When my mom first became ill in 2010, she wanted to ensure all of her personal affairs were in order. She made some preparations that I was not fully aware of until I sat in front of the funeral director. My mom was very specific and we had all of her documents in order. She was an extremely private person. Mom did not want a funeral service or an obituary. She requested that there be no viewing of her body. She chose not to be embalmed. She even picked out a casket and purchased a plot at her preferred cemetery. My mother had an insurance policy that covered the expenses of the goods and services she selected. I was able to provide the funeral home with the policy. I respectfully honored my mom's wishes, so I made no adjustments to her pre-arrangements. The balance of the policy was distributed according to my mom's request. The only thing we had to purchase was her grave marker.

I cannot begin to tell you how relieved I was when I walked into the funeral home she chose, with my mom's "Peace and Order" binder filled with her documents and requests. I cannot begin to tell you how relieved I was when I walked out stress-free, knowing that my mom had her personal matters in order. Talk about relief – with no stress! I was able to then grieve over the loss of my mother, my confidant, and my friend.

Everyone's desires are different. Some, unlike my mom, may want an elaborate home-going or celebration of life service. Now is the opportunity to put your desires in writing.

If you want a funeral or a certain type of memorial service - write it down! If you want to be cremated and have your ashes scattered on top of Mount Everest - write it down! If you want something specific in your obituary - write it down! Make known your favorite songs, poems, and/or scriptures. You may want to write your own program; some people have done this. You may have a special request for your family. Make sure your family knows what part your clergy, church, or religious organization is to play in the handling of your service. Be as specific as you can. You may not want a service of any kind – that is your prerogative; just make it known and write it down!

It may be your desire to donate your body for scientific research or to donate your organs for a possible transplant. Make sure you complete the proper documents with the state in which you reside, and that your family is aware of your preferences.

Additionally, if you have young dependents, you may want to specify who you desire to be their legal guardian. Appointment of guardianship should be done through a will, so make sure you have one in place. You will need to enlist the services of an attorney to ensure the legal validity of the documents.

As time goes on, some of this information may change, so I encourage you to make modifications annually or on an as needed basis. The most important point of this section, and this entire guide, is that you have something in writing to assist your family in preparing for your earthly departure.

Document as much information as you would like your family to have. Supply the following details:

Church/Chapel/Synagogue Preference – If you desire a specific location for your funeral service, make known to your family the name and location of the facility you wish to have your home-going celebration, memorial service, or funeral service. Supply an alternative location as a backup.

Religious Affiliation – If you are a part of a religious organization, please ensure your family is aware of any and all religious ceremonies you wish to have.

Clergy – Make sure your family has the name of your clergyperson and the role he or she will play in your requested services. Make certain that your cleric is made aware in advance of your preferences. A copy of your final wishes should be given to him or her as well, especially if they are to play a part in your ceremony.

Funeral Home - It is customary in some cultures that many families use the same funeral home. You may decide to use the same facility or you may not. In any case, inform your family your choice. Keep in mind the location of the funeral home in proximity to the other venues you may select.

Funeral Arrangements – Many funeral homes now offer pre-planning assistance. You have the option to pre-arrange and/or prepay for their services. Prices will vary for each service offered and also at each facility. By law, in many states, funeral directors must supply a price list to anyone who requests a copy. Ask for a copy so that you have an idea what their products and services may cost.

Burial - Do you prefer interment, entombment, or cremation? - Answering this question makes it clear to your family what you desire and it leaves no room for guessing. Some individuals have no preference, and others are very adamant about their choice.

Final Resting Place — Many families have a cemetery of choice in which their ancestors are buried. You may desire to keep that tradition or you may not. Oftentimes, families buy burial space to obtain a number of grave sites for several members of their family. Purchasing a burial space in advance allows you to secure the location you desire. Make it known where you would like your final resting place.

Have you purchased a burial plot, crypt, space in a mausoleum, or an urn? - The cost of plots varies by location; an idyllic location can be more expensive than a less desirable area. There are also options to have your final resting place in a mausoleum or crypt – burial above the ground. The cost of the mausoleum or crypt depends upon the cemetery. If you choose cremation, you also have the option to be buried in a cemetery. Similar to funeral homes, cemeteries must supply a list of products and services offered along with prices, upon request. When you prepay, make sure your family is aware of any additional fees such as the opening and closing of the grave.

Military Cemetery – Veterans or active duty personnel are eligible to be buried in a military cemetery. This may include their spouse and children. Verify eligibility of this benefit.

***

CHAPTER EIGHT

COUNTING THE COSTS

One thing you will find as you begin to preplan, even at the least expensive rate, funeral expenses can be very costly. The average total cost of a funeral in the United States, which includes funeral home, cemetery, and headstone or grave marker is roughly $8,000-$10,000. And, basic cremation with memorial service average cost is approximately $1,500-$3,000.

Whether you choose to prepay or have insurance for your final arrangements, you are encouraged to at least have something in place and someone should be advised.

If you have an insurance policy, please review it carefully to ensure that it is current and there are enough available funds to cover the projected cost of your arrangements. You have the option to purchase whole or term life insurance; the choice is often based upon what you can afford. It is important that you have some type of insurance or money set aside that covers not only your funeral expenses, but replaces your income if you are responsible for supporting your family.

Prepaying your burial expenses is another means of ensuring that your family is not scrambling to make ends meet when it comes to handling your arrangements. By prepaying you have the ability to state the type of services you desire, the casket or urn you desire, and how you want your remains to be handled. However, before prepaying, please make sure you are dealing with a reputable funeral home establishment. Read the fine lines. Make sure you understand exactly what you are prepaying for and what is not covered in your plan. Make sure you research your option. Most states have specific laws in place to protect funeral and burial prepayments.

An alternative to prepaying is working with a funeral director to pre-arrange your burial plans. Pre-arrangement allows you to select exactly what you desire; this includes the casket, whether you want to be embalmed, and all the other important details pertaining to your burial services. Once you know the approximate costs, you can make a deposit and set the remaining amount of money aside at a bank in a Payable-On-Death (POD) account that is designated for your funeral expenses. The money you set aside with the bank can be withdrawn, if necessary, and you can gain interest on the balance. You may name someone as beneficiary or add him or her to your account. This person has authority to withdraw the funds from your POD account immediately upon your death.

(Prices for burial plans are subject to change with the POD choice.)

Another option is to obtain an insurance policy to cover the approximate cost. When you pass away, that policy is submitted to the funeral home. The funeral home can also be named as beneficiary on that policy, if you wish. Work closely with a licensed insurance agent to choose the best option.

The next step is purchasing a cemetery plot. This is a good idea because you get to lock-in the price. Since costs increase annually, this could be a very desirable option. In addition, you secure your desired location. Again, read all the documents carefully to ensure you are aware of any additional costs, such as the opening and closing of the grave.

As you gather the information for your final wishes, you may realize that you have not given much thought to what is required to plan a funeral. However, this information is not only vital to your family, but to the establishments providing these services.

Oftentimes, senior citizens have many of these plans in place; however, the planning process is not limited to seniors. Everyone should consider making preparations; mainly because no one knows when he or she will depart from this earth. Seize the opportunity by *Leaving Peace and Order* for your family. By making these preparations ahead of time you are leaving your family an important gift - thus, your family can grieve without having to deal with the unnecessary stress of handling your affairs.

***

CHAPTER NINE

GATHERING AND RECORDING INFORMATION

You are going to create your own "Peace and Order" binder. The time it takes to complete these steps depends upon how much of your information you readily have available.

As I stated, you will be gathering, recording, and finally storing your information. Although some things will seem elementary, please continue with the process because it is important that all necessary information and documents are in place. You may also ask why you need to record this information if it is listed on the document. The recording aspect of this project is to ensure that you have at-a-glance access to your information, instead of having to sort through your documents to locate the information.

Go to my website, www.ivoryspossibilities.com, to download a free copy of the "Peace and Order" worksheets needed to complete this project.

Most of the information you are gathering can be used not only after you pass away, but during the course of your life. For instance: if you get married, you will need your birth certificate; if you purchase a home, you will need your financial information; if you get sick, you will need your medical history. Having your "Peace and Order" binder is not just for your family when you die; it can be vitally important and useful during your lifetime.

Now the first thing you must do is make a decision to complete the steps in this guide. Procrastination *(to put off or to defer until a later time; delay)* will be the demise of this project. Therefore, you are encouraged to complete the steps as you read the guide. Make an appointment with yourself, and/or with your family, making it a family project. As I stated, this would be an ideal time for open dialogue. Either way, you owe it to yourself and your family to get your personal affairs in order!

~~~

GET STARTED!

Now that you have stated your final wishes, it is time to start gathering and recording pertinent information. You will gather information for the following categories:

- Personal Information
- Family History
- Medical History
- Employment History
- Employer Benefits

- Personal Financial Information
- Creditor Information
- Real Estate and Property Information
- Insurance Information
- Retirement Information
- Password Information
- Living Will and Powers of Attorney
- Will or Living Trust
- Address Book
- Miscellaneous Information

You have the option to record your information on the "Peace and Order" worksheets or you may record your information on notebook paper, tablet or personal computer, if you are not comfortable using forms. The format in which you place your information is not important; just take time to record it.

~~~

1. PERSONAL INFORMATION

The first step to creating your "Peace and Order" binder is to actually sit down and record all your personal information.

Gather the following documents: birth certificate, social security card, passport, visa, green card, driver's license, state identification, marriage license, divorce documents, and any other documents which pertain to your personal information.

Record the following information: your legal name or alias, former names, birthdate, birth place, social security number, address, former addresses, phone numbers, and marital status. Include your state identification number, driver's license number, passport number and any other numbers pertaining to forms of identification. Although this information is on the items you gather, it is important that you enter it on the forms so that you have your information readily accessible in an at-a-glance format. Having your personal information in order and in one place can be a tremendous help to you and your family in various ways.

***

2. FAMILY HISTORY

Use this section to list your family history. List the names of your parents, spouse, children, grandparents, siblings, grandchildren, great grandchildren and so on. Family history is not only good for informational purposes, but it is useful for sharing history with your children's children. This list may include just your immediate family, or you may want to branch out to other relatives such as aunts, uncles, nieces, nephews, and cousins. You may have to pick up the phone and do a little research to compile this list. Keep in mind that this is a good list to have in your possession.

This section may take you a bit of time, but do not lose focus. Start with your immediate family and later go back and add other relatives to your list. For your immediate family, if you are married, list your spouse and your spouse's personal information. If you have a child or children, list name, date of birth, social security number, and address. Do the same for your step-children, adopted children, grandchildren, foster children, etc.

If you have given a child up for adoption or conceived a child outside of your marriage union, list as much information about that child as well. This may be a touchy subject and I am not passing judgment, but having this information documented can be vitally important. (Take this time to discuss this truth with your spouse.)

When documenting other relatives, you need only list their name, date of birth, place of birth, and contact information. Having this information can come in handy, so do take the time to go back and document as many relatives as you can.

***

3. MEDICAL HISTORY

This section is very important and should not be ignored. It is most useful if you have an illness, become ill and/or are unable to respond to questions regarding previous medical history. I found that having access to my mom's medical history and a complete list of the medications she took was very helpful, and used often when I took my mom to the doctor or to the emergency room.

Gather the contact information for the following: all of your current or previous medical professionals and facilities including: physicians, dentists, therapists, chiropractors, psychiatrists, hospitals, pharmacies, etc.

Record the following information: your name, date of birth, blood type, height, weight and sex. Then list the names of your medical professionals, type of practice, addresses, phone numbers, and any other information that would be helpful when contacting those individuals on your behalf. Please include your primary care physician and all other physicians attending you. Given the privacy laws in place, it is very important that you make sure these medical professionals have the name of at least one family member on file, with whom they can share your medical information.

List all past and present illnesses during the course of your life including: cancer, high blood pressure, diabetes, glaucoma, gallstones, kidney disease, anemia, stroke, sleep apnea, tumors, infectious diseases, etc.

Record all surgeries, procedures and times of hospitalization; and detail the results from each event. Make a list of your current immunizations and treatments. If you have allergies, please list all types. This list may include allergies to penicillin, surgical tape, latex gloves, etc.

It is also important that you keep a current list of all the medications and supplements you take on a regular basis. List each prescription, prescribing physician, frequency and dosage of all prescribed medications. Record the different supplements with the dosage that you take.

Additionally, include the medical history of your family; both mother and father's side, if you are privy to that information. This information is often requested by your attending physician, so make sure you are aware of the various types of diseases in your family bloodline and document them.

If you have children, dependents or elderly parents, for whom you are responsible, please take the time to gather and record their medical history as well.

***

4. EMPLOYMENT HISTORY

Make a list of your current and previous employers. You can go back as far as you wish. The idea is that you document all the employers for whom you have worked. However, it is more important that your current employer's information is documented and up-to-date. This information is imperative in case your family member needs to get in touch with the company where you are employed on your behalf.

Gather the following information: previous and current employment contact information.

Record the following information: employer(s) name, address, and phone number. Include position, hire date, employee number, your current supervisor's name and their contact information.

If you served or are serving in the military, please document all information pertaining to your service.

The information of your current and previous employment will help your family in determining who to notify regarding benefits you may have. That being said, let's move on to our next step.

***

5. EMPLOYER BENEFITS

Many companies offer employer benefits. These benefits include health insurance, life insurance, vacation, leave programs, investment plans, employee stock purchase plans, retirement plans, etc. You should be aware of any of these offerings you have and document them as well.

Gather all documents pertaining to: health insurance, life insurance, leave program, investment plans, retirement plans, etc.

Record the following information: type of health plan, type of life insurance plan, etc. List the type of health coverage plan(s) you have and whether it is for yourself only or a family plan. Include the plan and group number and know the amount of each deductible. It is important to know exactly what is covered in your insurance plan(s) and what is not.

If you have life insurance through your employer, list the insurance company, amount of coverage you have, and the names of your beneficiaries on the policy. Review your plans closely. Know exactly what your family is entitled to and what happens when you leave the company. When you leave your place of employment, it may be very costly to continue the company-supplied life insurance benefits. Therefore, you may want to obtain additional life insurance along with what your employer offers so that you have adequate insurance in place in case you leave or are terminated from your place of employment.

It is also good to document the amount of leave and vacation time you are entitled to at your place of employment. Recording this information will help your family in case you are hospitalized for a period of time or become disabled.

In this section, include the contact information for your company's Human Resources and/or Employee Benefits Services departments. Having this information readily accessible will make a world of difference.

**

6. PERSONAL FINANCIAL INFORMATION

Documenting your personal financial information is probably one of the most important steps to compiling your "Peace and Order" binder. Having this information in place can alleviate problems that could arise when it comes to your family handling your bank accounts, investments and other financial information.

Gather the following information: bank statements, safe deposit box number, investment account, stocks/bonds, retirement account and any other financial information you may have.

Record the following information: banking institution contact information, account number, beneficiary, names on joint account, safe deposit box number and location of key, investment account number, value, broker, investment institution contact information. Make sure you have documents for each of your accounts and record pertinent information from each document.

It is also very important that you name someone trustworthy to have access to your financial accounts. This person should be able to write checks or pay expenses on your behalf. Also make sure your beneficiary information is current on all your financial accounts, such as your investments, stocks and bonds, etc.

***

7. CREDITOR INFORMATION

We all have to pay someone for their services, whether we are debt-free or in debt. Taking the time to list your creditors is not only helpful to your family, but gives you an opportunity to assess and make plans to eliminate as much debt as you possibly can. Debt elimination helps alleviate the stress of having your family handle your financial affairs.

I encourage you to take the time to obtain a copy of your credit report and credit score. You may retrieve your free credit report online from AnnualCreditReport.com and your free credit score from CreditKarma.com. Your credit report will list many of your creditors and the amounts you owe them. Please review your credit report carefully and dispute any discrepancies you may find.

Gather the following information: mortgage loan, rent, credit card statements, utility bills, bank loans, auto loans, personal loans, etc.

Record the following information: name, account number, balance, and estimated payoff time for each creditor.

List the names of individuals to whom you owe money; include the amount and any interest to be paid. List also the names of individuals who owe *you* money along with the amount and any interest to be paid. Note whether you forgive the debt owed to you upon your death.

I worked closely with my mother to ensure she had no lingering debt. I also had a detailed list of all her creditors. When my mom passed away, I was able to contact all the utility companies to terminate the services. I cancelled her credit card immediately, which did not have a balance. Having my mom's creditors' information was an efficient way to ensure that I handled her financial affairs.

***

8. REAL ESTATE AND PERSONAL PROPERTY INFORMATION

Gather the following information: property deed, title, receipts, etc. for all the valuable property you own.

Record the following information: type of property, property owner(s), mortgage balance of property, value of property, lien on property, etc.

It is very important to document the type of ownership you have for your real estate property. Information such as whether you are the sole owner, joint owner, or tenant in common owner is important in transferring property to someone else. If you own property jointly with someone, when you die, that property goes directly to the other owner. If you are a tenant in common, then your percentage of ownership of the property goes to your heirs when you pass away. Make sure you understand the difference and type of ownership you have in place for your real estate.

If you have automobiles or other motor vehicles, list the following information: make/model, year, vehicle identification number (VIN), registration information, ownership status, title, etc.

In this technology age, we possess all types of expensive electronic gadgets including: mobile phones, televisions, stereos, computers, notebooks, iPads, etc. Gather the receipts and record the following information about your devices: item, cost, store, serial number and value of the item.

Document all valuables you may have such as expensive jewelry, furs, collector items, paintings, coins, stamps, etc. List the type of item and its value. Having this information may come in handy, especially if you are unfortunately robbed or the property is damaged.

***

9. INSURANCE INFORMATION

Gather the following information: all insurance policies including auto, home, life, health, disability, long-term care, etc.

Record the following information: policy number, insurance company and agent, term of the policy, beneficiaries, co-pays, and deductibles.

Take time to review all your insurance policies. Know exactly what is covered and what is not covered and the expiration dates and value of each policy. Most insurance options are obtained through your employer. Make sure you review and modify your policies, as needed, annually.

If you are working with a personal insurance agent, make sure he or she is licensed and trustworthy. Again, review and know what you are paying for and what you are entitled to receive in the end.

The recommended insurance policies everyone should have are life, health, automobile, homeowner/rental, and long-term disability. Make sure you shop around to get the options which best meet your needs.

Insurance coverage is very important. In some states, you are required to have specific types of insurance. So, please make certain you are properly insured.

The United States Government also offers health insurance programs such as Medicare and Medicaid. Medicare is federal health insurance that covers some hospital and medical expenses for individuals who are 65 years or older, and to persons of any age who have long-term disabilities. Medicaid is a medical and health services program for individuals of any age who fall within the low-income bracket. Depending upon the state, Medicaid is offered to those who are on public assistance. If you are utilizing either Medicare or Medicaid, please document all relevant information including identification number or group number.

In 2010, President Barak Obama signed The Affordable Care Act. This law aims to improve the health care system in the United States. Its goal is to broaden the health care coverage to more Americans, as well as protect individuals who currently hold health insurance policies. Effective 2014, most individuals in the United States must have health care coverage. If they do not, they may be required to pay a fee known as the "individual shared responsibility payment." To learn more about the Health Insurance Marketplace, your options, eligibility and the requirements, you may visit the HealthCare.gov.

***

10. RETIREMENT INFORMATION

Saving for retirement may sometimes seem impossible. However, it is very important that you save for the future.

Gather the following information: documents pertaining to your Social Security, IRA(s), Roth IRA(s), 401(k) plans, annuities, investments, stocks, bonds, etc.

Record the following information: banking, broker, and/or investment institution's contact information, account number, beneficiary, name if joint account, and value. Make sure you have documents for each of your accounts and record pertinent information for each one.

It is also important that you understand the tax implications of early withdrawal in some retirement savings plans. Having a retirement savings plan in place will determine the standard of living which you are accustomed. People are living and working longer, so saving for retirement at an early age allows you to accumulate more life savings for when you plan to retire.

***

11. PASSWORD INFORMATION

Another important area of information gathering, recording, and storing is your passwords. As I stated, we live in the age of technology and much of our personal business transactions are managed through the Internet. Banking, online bill pay, social media and other account information require passwords when managed through the Internet. The amount of passwords and account numbers we must maintain can become daunting. Having your passwords and account numbers in one place is not only helpful to you, but can be useful to your family if something were to happen to you.

Gather the following: website name, website address, type of account, account number, and password for each online account.

Record the following information: all of the account information including name, site address, account type, account number, password, security question and answer for each of your online accounts.

Many electronic gadgets such as phones, computers, notebooks, iPads, etc. require password or log-in information; document the type of device and its log-in and password information.

Do not forget to document combination numbers for safes and lockboxes you may have or use.

Numerous passwords are used at your place of employment. Make sure you include a list of all your log-in and password information. Some companies have the capability to reset your password; however, if you work for a small organization, access to your company passwords may not be easily obtained. Having your work log-in and password information documented will make it more convenient for your employer to access the information you manage if something were to happen to you.

***

12. LIVING WILL AND POWER OF ATTORNEY

A Living Will and Power of Attorney (for health and property) are also very important document that you should have in your file.

A Living Will allows you to legally give your physician advance healthcare directives concerning life support procedures. If you have a terminal medical condition or become incapacitated and are unable to communicate your healthcare treatment desires, having a living will in place legally communicates your wishes in advance. Your primary care physician should also have a copy of your living will.

The Power of Attorney for health allows you to grant a trusted individual (agent), usually a family member or friend, the power to make healthcare decisions on your behalf. If you become physically or mentally incapacitated, the agent will speak on your behalf, based upon your desired wishes stated in your power of attorney document. For instance, if you do or do not want to have your life prolonged on life support, you can state this in your power of attorney for health, and your agent will make sure your wishes are granted.

This document is in effect as long as you deem so and becomes obsolete upon your death.

The Power of Attorney for property is similar to the power of attorney for health. This document allows you to grant a trusted individual (agent), usually a family member or friend, the power to make decisions regarding your finances, bank accounts, assets, real estate, and other types of property that you may have. Based upon your wishes regarding your property, the agent will speak on your behalf if you become physically or mentally incapacitated. Again, this document is in effect as long as you deem so and becomes obsolete upon your death.

The advantages of having a power of attorney for property is that it gives you the ability to decide in advance who will make financial decisions for you in the event you are unable to make them for yourself.

Both the powers of attorney for health and property can be written by an attorney. You can also download and complete the forms from your state's website free of charge. Additionally, you must ensure the documents are notarized and witnessed.

Gather the following documents: living will, power of attorney for health, and power of attorney for property.

Record the following information: attorney's name, agent(s') names, document expiration date (if applicable), and contact information of the individual(s) you selected as power(s) of attorney.

Also in this section, you may state whether you would like to donate your organs. You can be specific as to which organs you would like to donate. You can also state whether you want your organs donated for transplant or scientific research purposes.

**

13. WILL OR LIVING TRUST

If you have children, property, or anything of value, I recommend that you consult an attorney to see if you need to execute a will and/or living trust. There are software packages you can purchase or downloadable forms online which allow you to create your own will. However, to ensure legality, it is better to have your will and/or living trust written by an attorney.

Having a will and/or living trust in place gives your family control of your property and specifies who should be guardian(s) of your children, rather than leaving the decision to the state in which you live. A will and/or living trust allows you to specify how you want your property distributed and to whom.

Everyone should consider obtaining a will and/or living trust. Please consult an estate planning attorney to assist you in completing your will and/or living trust.

***

14. ADDRESS BOOK

Family and friends' contact information may be stored in various places. Take time to print your address book from all of your electronic devices and store a copy in your "Peace and Order" binder. Also make sure that the information in your address books is current and up-to-date.

***

15. MISCELLANEOUS

Another item to store in your "Peace and Order" binder is a copy of the contents in your wallet. Take all the cards in your wallet, including your driver's license, and make a photo copy of them fitting as many as you can on a page. Copy both front and back of your driver's license and each card. Having this information is essential, especially if your wallet is lost or stolen. You do not have to panic because you know exactly what was in your wallet, and you also have the telephone numbers to cancel all of your credit cards and bank debit card. Make sure you take time to copy the contents in your wallet; it may prevent you from having your identity stolen.

Also use this section to store any other personal important documents not previously listed: such as letters, pictures, obituaries of family and friends, etc.

Think of a loved one going through your "Peace and Order" binder when you are gone, include any other information that you feel would be relevant, encouraging, enlightening, etc. You may even want to include an apology letter to someone -

however, I strongly advise that you apologize to the individual while you are both alive.

Use your binder to **leave peace and order** for the ones you love.

***

CHAPTER TEN

STORING YOUR INFORMATION

Now that you gathered and recorded your information for all the categories, it is time to store it.

You will need the following:

- Three-ring binder
- Clear plastic sheet protectors
- Divider tabs
- "Peace and Order" worksheets

Type all of your pertinent information you gathered onto the "Peace and Order" worksheets. The sheets are sectioned into 15 categories for ease-of-use. Once completed, save a copy of the form on your computer and on an external drive to be placed in your "Peace and Order" binder. Print a completed copy of the worksheets and place a copy in your "Peace and Order" binder and give a copy to a trusted family member or friend.

Now that you have collected (recorded) all of your important documents needed for your "Peace and Order" binder, it is time to get organized! Begin by placing each document into a clear plastic sheet protector and place each sheet in the binder under the appropriate category. For instance, all of the documents you gathered for your Personal Information section (i.e., birth certificate, marriage license, passport, etc.) should be placed individually in a clear plastic sheet protector behind the tab labeled or assigned for Personal Information. Complete this step for all 15 categories.

There should be a total of at least 15 sections with tabs for each category including a tab for miscellaneous items in your "Peace and Order" binder. Each tab should be designated for one of the 15 categories. Clear sheet protectors should be used to collect your important documents for each category. (This may vary slightly given your personal situation.)

Now that you have everything gathered, recorded, and stored in your "Peace and Order" binder, I also recommend that you purchase a fireproof/water resistant portable safe to keep your binder and other valuables.

It is up to you to designate one or two trusted individuals to have copies or access to the content in your "Peace and Order" binder.

***

THE INFORMATION YOU GATHER IS VERY SENSITIVE AND SHOULD BE HANDLED AND STORED AS SAFELY AS POSSIBLE. IDENTITY THEFT IS ON THE RISE, AND OFTEN OCCURS BY SOMEONE WE KNOW. THEREFORE, PLEASE ENSURE THAT YOU KEEP YOUR INFORMATION CONFIDENTIAL AND SHARE IT ONLY WITH THE TRUSTED INDIVIDUAL(S) YOU SELECT TO HANDLE YOUR AFFAIRS.

***

CHAPTER ELEVEN

FINAL WORD

Whew...that was a lot of information. This project of *Leaving Peace and Order* for your family may seem a bit overwhelming, but I encourage you to...DO IT ANYWAY!!! Once you complete this task you will be relieved and your family will appreciate it even more. This is one of the greatest gifts you can leave for your loved ones.

I cannot stress enough, how important it is to have your affairs together. When you have your personal business in order, you are giving your family an ultimate gift of *Leaving Peace and Order*!

I ask that you encourage others to read this guide and get their affairs in order. It is important to everyone and will ease the burdens of your loved ones in the end.

***

CHAPTER TWELVE

WHAT OTHERS ARE SAYING

*"When I retired two years ago, I realized that my finances would be difficult for my children to deal with when I passed on and that I needed to put my affairs in order. I hesitated because I did not really know where to start. **Leaving Peace and Order!**, for me, is the answer to a prayer I had not yet uttered. It is amazingly detailed and comprehensive. The personal details of why it was written are spiritually uplifting enough to motivate me to start the task right away. I am looking forward to completing it and do not dread the research I will have to do to make sure it is complete.*

Reading the book and completing the tasks are an absolute "MUST DO". It is a gift from God, a divine gift left to those of us still alive by the author's mother. I am sure once you read it; you will be as inspirited as I am now."

Mary Louise Wicks, Ph.D.
Former Senior Administrator of Student
Support Services
Orange County Public School System
Orlando, FL

***

*"**Leaving Peace and Order** is a guide filled with information that no one should be without. It is truly an eye opener, a must read for everyone. Even as one in the medical profession who had to talk to patients about living wills and other legal matters, I learned many things I would never have thought about from this guide. It helped me to do*

some serious thinking and make some important decisions. Contained in this book is very valuable information that every family needs, and should have."

Armorie Lee
Retired RN at Veteran's Hospital
Waukegan, IL

***

*"The guide "**Leaving Peace and Order!**" is an AMAZING and AWESOME resource/guide. The author Kimberly Ivory Graves did an outstanding job putting this guide together. I've known Kimberly since 1983 and it doesn't surprise me that this guide is in fruition and was masterminded by her. Having the motivation to move this project forward is just a small aspect of her dedication to God, family and friends.*

As I read through the guide, I was amazed that she covered every detail in some aspect of what I went through personally not having any Peace and Order when my loved ones passed away. The process can be so overwhelming, but this guide will help minimize that stress. I expect to share the guide personally with family and friends; with full intentions that it will make the inevitable process of losing your loved ones at least peaceful.

I personally thank Kimberly Ivory Graves for all of her prayers for me and sharing this guide ***"Leaving Peace and Order!"***

Delphia M. Esters
Prairie View, TX

***

"Kimberly, thanks so much for following through on this project-vision that God has placed on your heart to do. You wrote the vision and made it plain in the development and implementation of this great guide for all of us that know that this type of stewardship needs to be done now rather than after the fact when our love ones or we ourselves make our transition home to be with our Lord and Savior Jesus Christ. I pray that you will continue to implement the project-visions that God gives you to help others in getting their house in order in a peaceful way and connecting to His word - (Habakkuk 2:2)"

Cynthia R. Dockery-Harris, CMP
Executive Director of Meetings and Events
Meeting Essentials By D'esign, Inc.
Waukegan, IL

***

EPILOGUE

Now that you are encouraged and inspired to get your affairs in order, I would like to seriously admonish you to make one final preparation. As I have shown you, death is inevitable. The Bible says in Hebrews 9:27 *"And as it is appointed unto men once to die; but after this the judgment;"*

We all must stand before God, our Creator, and give an account for the things done here on Earth. There is life after death on Earth. This life is either eternity with Jesus Christ or eternal damnation in hell's fire. You must make the decision and choose which life you desire. And actually, the choice is quite simple. No one wants to spend eternity separated from God in hell's fire. So choose life through Jesus Christ.

If you are ready to make the right choice, pray this simple life changing prayer:

Father, in the name of Jesus, I come to you <u>acknowledging</u> that I am a sinner lost without you. I <u>believe</u> that you sent your son Jesus to die on Calvary's cross and he rose again for my sins. I repent and turn away from all my sins and ask that you forgive me and cleanse me in the precious blood of Jesus. I <u>confess</u> that Jesus is Lord and today I receive Him as my Lord and Savior. I choose abundant life here on earth and eternal life with Jesus Christ. It is in Jesus' name that I pray and believe it is so. Amen!

"But what saith it? The word is nigh thee, even in thy mouth, and in thy heart: that is, the word of faith, which we preach; That if thou shalt confess with thy mouth the Lord Jesus, and shalt believe in

thine heart that God hath raised him from the dead, thou shalt be saved. For with the heart man believeth unto righteousness; and with the mouth confession is made unto salvation. For the scripture saith, Whosoever believeth on him shall not be ashamed. For there is no difference between the Jew and the Greek: for the same Lord over all is rich unto all that call upon him. For whosoever shall call upon the name of the Lord shall be saved." (Romans 10:8-13)

Welcome to the family of God!

Send us a note to let us know of your decision to make Jesus Christ, Lord of your life. Visit www.ivoryspossibilities.com.

ABOUT THE AUTHOR

Kimberly Ivory Graves has a passion for helping people and she turned that passion into what she loves most - assisting individuals to get organized and out of debt. Kimberly founded *Ivory's Possibilities*, a personal organizer and budget coaching business. Kimberly conducts personal finance budgeting and organizing classes individually, as well as in group settings.

Kimberly earned her Bachelor of Science degree in Financial Services and Accounting from Columbia College of Missouri where she graduated as Magna Cum Laude. Kimberly has over 20 years of administrative and organizational experience.

Kimberly is a ghost writer and first-time author and publisher.

Kimberly Ivory Graves resides in Northern Illinois with her husband Douglas Graves.

To learn more about Ivory's Possibilities and Kimberly Ivory Graves, visit:

www.ivoryspossibilities.com